Healthy Eating

A Balanced Diet

Catherine Veitch

Raintree

www.raintreepublishers.co.uk
Visit our website to find out more information about Raintree books.

To order:
Phone 0845 6044371
Fax +44 (0) 1865 312263
Email myorders@raintreepublishers.co.uk

Customers from outside the UK please telephone +44 1865 312262

Raintree is an imprint of Capstone Global Library Limited, a company incorporated in England and Wales having its registered office at 7 Pilgrim Street, London, EC4V 6LB – Registered company number: 6695582

First published in hardback in 2012
First published in paperback in 2013

Edited by Daniel Nunn, Rebecca Rissman, and Harriet Milles
Designed by Joanna Hinton-Malivoire
Picture research by Elizabeth Alexander
Originated by Capstone Global Library Ltd.
Production by Victoria Fitzgerald
Printed and bound in China by Leo Paper Products Ltd

ISBN 978 1 406 22898 4 (hardback)
15 14 13 12 11
10 9 8 7 6 5 4 3 2 1

ISBN 978 1 406 22961 5 (paperback)
16 15 14 13 12
10 9 8 7 6 5 4 3 2 1

British Library Cataloguing in Publication Data
Veitch, Catherine.
A balanced diet. – (Acorn plus)
1. Nutrition–Pictorial works–Juvenile literature.
2. Food–Pictorial works–Juvenile literature.
3. Health–Pictorial works–Juvenile literature.
I. Title II. Series
613.2-dc22
A full catalogue record for this book is available from the British Library.

Acknowledgements
We would like to thank the following for permission to reproduce photographs: © Capstone Publishers **p. 4** (Karon Dubke); Getty Images **pp. 14** (Jeffrey Coolidge/The Image Bank), **22e** (Jeffrey Coolidge/The Image Bank); Food Standards Agency/ © Crown copyright material is reproduced with the permission of the Controller of HMSO and Queen's Printer for Scotland **p. 5**; iStockphoto **pp. 7** (© Linda Kloosterhof), **15** (© Nathan Marx); Photolibrary **pp. 8 left** (Gary k Smith), **12** (VIDAL VIDAL), **19** (Corbis); Shutterstock **pp. 6 left** (© Mikael Damkier), **6 top right** (© Uwe Pilla), **6 bottom right, 22a** (© BestPhoto1), **8 right, 22b** (© bornholm), **9** (© Monkey Business Images), **10, 22c** (© MarFot), **10 inset** (© Matka_Wariatka), **11, 13** (© Morgan Lane Photography), **12 inset, 22d** (© Lana Langlois), **16 top left** (© LockStockBob),**16 top right** (© raliand), **16 bottom left** (© Stephen Orsillo),**16 bottom right** (© Peter Kirillov), **17, 22f** (© Olga Miltsova), **18 top left** (© Svetlana Lukienko), **18 top right** (© Elnur), **18 bottom left** (© taesmileland), **18 bottom right** (© val lawless), **20** (© Mandy Godbehear), **21** (© Gabriel Nardelli Araujo).

Front cover photograph of a boy eating a sandwich reproduced with permission of Corbis (© Jose Luis Pelaez, Inc./Blend Images). Back cover photograph of a nutritious plate of food © Capstone Publishers (Karon Dubke).

We would like to thank Sarah Schenker for her invaluable help in the preparation of this book.

Contents

Some words appear in bold, **like this**. You can find out what they mean in "Words to know" on page 23.

A balanced diet

A **balanced diet** includes fruit, vegetables, **starchy foods**, milk and **dairy foods**, meat, fish, eggs, and beans.

The **eatwell plate** shows us the main food groups. You need to eat food from these food groups and get plenty of exercise to keep your body healthy.

Fruit

Fruit grows on plants. Apples, tomatoes, and raspberries are fruits. Apples grow on trees. Some tomatoes grow on vines. Raspberries grow on bushes. Eating fruit helps your body fight illness and keeps you healthy.

Most fruits can be picked and eaten as they are. Sometimes fruits are squeezed and made into juice. Most children need to eat 5 servings of fruit and vegetables each day.

Vegetables

A vegetable is a type of plant. Carrots and peas are vegetables. Carrots grow under the ground. Peas grow above the ground. Eating vegetables helps keep your body healthy.

Some vegetables can be picked and eaten as they are. Some vegetables are cooked. Most children need to eat 5 servings of vegetables and fruit each day.

Starchy foods

Starchy foods include pasta, bread, potatoes, and food made from **grains**. Grains are the seeds from some plants. Oats, wheat, and rice are grains. Eating starchy foods gives you **energy** and keeps you healthy.

We make some grains into flour. Bread, pasta, and buns are made from flour. Other grains, such as rice, are cooked in water. Make sure that at least half of the grains you eat are made from whole grains.

Milk and dairy foods

Cows make milk. Many farmers use machines to take milk from the cows. They take the milk to a **dairy**. Machines at the dairy prepare the milk. Then the milk is put into bottles or cartons.

Milk can be made into **dairy foods**. Cheese and yoghurt are dairy foods. Eating dairy foods helps build strong bones and teeth.

Meat, fish, eggs, and beans

Meat is a food that comes from animals such as cows, pigs, and chickens. Meat, fish, and eggs give you **protein**. Other foods that give you protein are beans and nuts.

Most meat is cooked before it can be eaten. It is important to cook meat well. Eating protein helps you to grow.

Healthy fats

Some fats in our food are good for us. Some fats are bad for us if we eat too much of them. Healthy fats are found in fish, seeds, nuts, and plants. Unhealthy fats are found in cakes, biscuits, and fried food.

Oils are fats. Some oils come from vegetables or seeds. Some people use oil when they cook food. Oils can also be used on salads. Eating some of these oils helps you fight illness and stay healthy.

Sugar

There is a lot of sugar in biscuits, sweets, fizzy drinks, and cakes. Too much sugar is bad for your body. To keep your body healthy, you should try to eat only small amounts of sugar.

Too much sugar is bad for your teeth. It is important to brush your teeth after eating sugary foods. You need to clean the sugar from your teeth.

Exercise and sleep

As well as eating a **balanced diet**, your body needs regular **exercise**. Regular exercise helps build strong bones and muscles, and a healthy heart.

Your body also needs to rest. Sleep helps you stay strong and healthy. Most children need between 10 and 12 hours of sleep each night.

Can you remember?

a

b

c

d

e

f

Can you guess which food groups these foods belong to? Look back through the book if you need help.

Answers on page 24

Words to know

balanced diet diet that includes food from all the food groups. A balanced diet helps keep a body healthy and fit.

dairy place where butter and cheese are made from milk

dairy food food made from milk. Cheese, yoghurt, butter, and cream are dairy foods.

eatwell plate the eatwell plate shows us what foods to eat to stay healthy

energy power to do something. We need energy when we work or play.

exercise physical activity that helps keep a body healthy and fit

grains seeds of some plants. Wheat and rice are grains.

oil fat in food

protein substance in food that gives the body energy and helps it grow. Eggs, meat, nuts, and beans have protein in them.

starchy food food that gives the body energy. Pasta, cereals, and bread are starchy foods.

Index

Answers to quiz on page 22:
a) fruit b) vegetables c) starchy foods d) milk e) meat f) fat

Notes for parents and teachers

Before reading

Show the children the photo of the eatwell plate on p. 4. Guide children in a discussion about what "balanced" means. Then explain that a balanced diet includes food from all the food groups. Tell children they will learn about the main food groups.

After reading

- As a shared task with the class, write down as many foods as the children can think of in each food group. Ask children if they can think of any foods that are not so healthy.
- Bring in a selection of food magazines (such as free supermarket magazines). Ask children to find and cut out pictures of foods from different food groups and put them in separate piles. Give each child a paper plate and ask them to select a picture from each pile to put on their plates to make a healthy meal. Make a wall display of the children's healthy meals.